॥ SAPPHO

SAPPHO
A NEW TRANSLATION

by
MARY BARNARD

Foreword by Dudley Fitts

UNIVERSITY OF CALIFORNIA PRESS
BERKELEY, LOS ANGELES, LONDON

UNIVERSITY OF CALIFORNIA PRESS
Berkeley and Los Angeles, California

UNIVERSITY OF CALIFORNIA PRESS, LTD.
London, England

© 1958 by The Regents of the University of California
© renewed 1986 by Mary Barnard
ISBN 978-0-520-22312-7
Library of Congress Catalog Card Number: 58-6520

Designed by Adrian Wilson
Printed in the United States of America

15   14   13   12   11   10   09   08   07
14   13   12   11   10   9   8   7   6

The paper used in this publication meets the minimum
requirements of ANSI/NISO Z39.48-1992 (R 1997)
(*Permanence of Paper*). ♾

回 To Douglas and Marie Paige
in return for the little volume
of *Lirici Greci*

◨ FOREWORD

In one of her fragments Sappho says, or seems to say,
that men in time to come will remember her. So much
is any poet's permissible hope, that

> non omnis moriar, magnaque pars mei
> vitabit Libitinam,

yet of few poets has it come more uncomfortably true.
Who is Sappho? A lyrist unparalleled, a great beauty,
no great beauty, a rumor, a writer of cultist hymns,
a scandal, a fame, a bitchy sister to a silly brother, a
headmistress, a mystic, a mistress of the poet Alkaios,
a pervert, a suicide for love of a ferryman, an an-
drogyne, a bluestocking, a pretty mother of a prettier
daughter, an avatar of Yellow Book neodiabolism; a
Greek. We can agree to "lyrist" and "Greek," partic-
ularising the latter as sixth century and Lesbian, and
basing the former on the evidence of two nearly in-
tact poems and a number of fragments. The rest is
speculation, when it is not something less savory, and
neither the gossip of scandalmongers nor the scru-

pulous research of scholars should cause us to forget
that it is nothing but speculation. We have heard a
great deal about Sappho, and we know almost noth-
ing. The sands of Egypt have been generous and
papyruses are still being found, but unless we are
granted a discovery of almost theophanic import we
are not likely to learn much more.

Yet a reputation like Sappho's· can not be wholly
the result of accident. The ancient writers who knew
her work agreed that she was a poet of the first im-
portance. The scandal that attaches itself to her may
have been popularized by the writers of Middle Com-
edy, but scandal of this sort does not gravitate towards
a nonentity. Moreover, the testimony of the two pre-
served odes argues an idiosyncratic, almost inimitable
power, and even "devouring Time" has been most kind
in the very act of devouring: for there is this to be
said for fragmentary survival, that no one can prove
that you didn't write brilliantly, and an ingenious
partisan can make it apparent that you did. A certain
radiance may invest even the meanest of your remain-
ing shreds; so that when an old commentator writes

> At the porch the most musical and μειλιχόφωνοι
> [gentle-voiced] of the girls sang the marriage an-
> them, which clearly is Sappho's most delicate com-
> position,

a word not otherwise notable can become germinally
suggestive, a toy for the imagination. From the tiny
part we are tempted to imagine the whole: a generous
exercise, if we remember that it is intended as nothing

more conclusive, and one that is admirably rewarding
in Miss Barnard's book.

What I chiefly admire in Miss Barnard's transla-
tions and reconstructions is the direct purity of diction
and versification. There are perilous guesses, auda-
cious twists, and inevitable flights to the authority of
intuition alone; but there is no spurious poeticism,
none of the once so fashionable Swinburne-Symonds
erethism provoked by

> The small dark body's Lesbian loveliness
> That held the fire eternal.

(I think it did, by the way.) What Miss Barnard per-
ceives, and what no one would ever have guessed
from the general run of talk about Sappho, is the
pungent downright plain style. An excellent example
is the beginning of fragment 16 (Miss Barnard's 41):

> Some say a cavalry corps,
> some infantry, some, again,
> will maintain that the swift oars
>
> of our fleet are the finest
> sight on dark earth; but I say
> that whatever one loves, is.

I do not see how that could be bettered. Like the
Greek, it is stripped and hard, awkward with the fine
awkwardness of truth. Here is no trace of the "sweete
slyding, fit for a verse" that one expects to find in
renderings of Sappho. It is exact translation; but in
its composition, the spacing, the arrangement of
stresses, it is also high art. This, one thinks, is what

Sappho must have been like; and Longinus, or who-ever wrote that famous treatise *De Sublimitate,* was no fool when he pointed.to her marshaling of sharp details, rather than to the melody of her verse, as the secret of her eloquence. Antipoetry, one may say; but it may be that antipoetry is what one needs, if it im-plies the discarding of gauds and ornamental tropes, the throwing overboard of the whole apparatus of factitious "beauty" that has for so long attached itself to the name of Sappho of Lesbos.

DUDLEY FITTS

⚙ CONTENTS

PART SIX

98. It is the Muses
99. Must I remind you, Cleis
100. I have no complaint

Tell everyone

Now, today, I shall
sing beautifully for
my friends' pleasure

彡 2   We shall enjoy it

As for him who finds
fault, may silliness
and sorrow take him!

◙ PART ONE

℞ 3   Standing by my bed

In gold sandals
Dawn that very
moment awoke me

꧰ 4   I asked myself

What, Sappho, can
you give one who
has everything,
like Aphrodite?

꧰ 5   And I said

I shall burn the
fat thigh-bones of
a white she-goat
on her altar

6   I confess

I love that
which caresses
me. I believe

Love has his
share in the
Sun's brilliance
and virtue

At noontime

When the earth is
bright with flaming
heat falling straight down

the cricket sets
up a high-pitched
singing in his wings

□ 8   I took my lyre and said:

Come now, my heavenly
tortoise shell: become
a speaking instrument

□ 9   Although they are

Only breath, words
which I command
are immortal

𐤀 10   That afternoon

Girls ripe to marry
wove the flower-
heads into necklaces

𐤀 11   We heard them chanting:

FIRST
VOICE   Young Adonis is
dying! O Cytherea
What shall we do now?

SECOND
VOICE   Batter your breasts
with your fists, girls—
tatter your dresses!

□ 12   It's no use

Mother dear, I
can't finish my
weaving
          You may
blame Aphrodite

soft as she is

she has almost
killed me with
love for that boy

回 13   People do gossip

          And they say about
          Leda, that she

          once found an egg
          hidden under

          wild hyacinths

℡ 14   Peace reigned in heaven

Ambrosia stood
already mixed
in the wine bowl

It was Hermes
who took up the
wine jug and poured
wine for the gods

℡ 15   When I saw Eros

On his way down
from heaven, he

wore a soldier's
cloak dyed purple

16   You are the herdsman of evening

Hesperus, you herd
homeward whatever
Dawn's light dispersed

You herd sheep—herd
goats—herd children
home to their mothers

🄿 17   Sleep, darling

I have a small
daughter called
Cleis, who is

like a golden
flower
        I wouldn't
take all Croesus'
kingdom with love
thrown in, for her

Although clumsy

Mnasidica has a more
shapely figure than
our gentle Gyrinno

℔ 19 　　　Tomorrow you had better

Use your soft hands,
Dica, to tear off
dill shoots, to cap
your lovely curls

She who wears flowers
attracts the happy
Graces: they turn
back from a bare head

20   We put the urn aboard ship
with this inscription:

This is the dust of little
Timas who unmarried was led
into Persephone's dark bedroom

And she being far from home, girls
her age took new-edged blades
to cut, in mourning for her,
these curls of their soft hair

Cyprian, in my dream

The folds of a purple
kerchief shadowed
your cheeks—the one

Timas one time sent,
a timid gift, all
the way from Phocaea

In the spring twilight

The full moon is shining:
Girls take their places
as though around an altar

And their feet move

Rhythmically, as tender
feet of Cretan girls
danced once around an

altar of love, crushing
a circle in the soft
smooth flowering grass

Awed by her splendor

Stars near the lovely
moon cover their own
bright faces
                when she
is roundest and lights
earth with her silver

Now, while we dance

Come here to us
gentle Gaiety,
Revelry, Radiance

and you, Muses
with lovely hair

PART TWO

Epithalamia

26 The evening star

Is the most
beautiful
of all stars

回 27 It is time now

FIRST VOICE For you who are so
pretty and charming

to share in games
that the pink-ankled
Graces play, and

gold Aphrodite

O never!

SECOND VOICE I shall be a
virgin always

For her sake

We ask you
to come now

O Graces O
rosy-armed
perfection:

God's daughters

⊡ 29   *Hymen Hymenaon!*

FIRST   Raise the rafters! Hoist
VOICE   them higher! Here comes
         a bridegroom taller
         than Ares!

SECOND   *Hymen*
VOICE   *Hymenaon!*

FIRST   He towers
VOICE   above tall men as
         poets of Lesbos
         over all others!

SECOND   *Sing Hymen*
VOICE   *O Hymenaon*

We drink your health

Lucky bridegroom!
Now the wedding you
asked for is over

and your wife is the
girl you asked for;
she's a bride who is

charming to look at,
with eyes as soft as
honey, and a face

that Love has lighted
with his own beauty.
Aphrodite has surely

outdone herself in
doing honor to you!

Bridesmaids' carol I

O Bride brimful of
rosy little loves!

O brightest jewel of
the Queen of Paphos!

Come now
           to your
bedroom   to your
bed
     and play there
sweetly   gently
with your bridegroom

And may Hesperus
lead you not at all
unwilling
           until
you stand wondering
before the silver

Throne of Hera
Queen of Marriage

FIRST
VOICE   Virginity O
          my virginity!

          Where will you
          go when I lose
          you?
SECOND   I'm off to
VOICE   a place I shall
          never come back
          from
                Dear Bride!
          I shall never
          come back to you

              Never!

℞ 33   They're locked in, oh!

The doorkeeper's
feet are twelve
yards long! ten shoe-

makers used five
oxhides to cobble
sandals for them!

Lament for a maidenhead

FIRST
VOICE
Like a quince-apple
ripening on a top
branch in a tree top

not once noticed by
harvesters or if
not unnoticed, not reached

SECOND
VOICE
Like a hyacinth in
the mountains, trampled
by shepherds until
only a purple stain
remains on the ground

🏳 35   You wear her livery

Shining with gold,
you, too, Hecate,
Queen of Night, hand-
maid to Aphrodite

🏳 36   Why am I crying?

Am I still sad
because of my
lost maidenhead?

◫ PART THREE

You know the place: then

Leave Crete and come to us
waiting where the grove is
pleasantest, by precincts

sacred to you; incense
smokes on the altar, cold
streams murmur through the

apple branches, a young
rose thicket shades the ground
and quivering leaves pour

down deep sleep; in meadows
where horses have grown sleek
among spring flowers, dill

scents the air. Queen! Cyprian!
Fill our gold cups with love
stirred into clear nectar

Prayer to my lady of Paphos

Dapple-throned Aphrodite,
eternal daughter of God,
snare-knitter! Don't, I beg you,

cow my heart with grief! Come,
as once when you heard my far-
off cry and, listening, stepped

from your father's house to your
gold car, to yoke the pair whose
beautiful thick-feathered wings

oaring down mid-air from heaven
carried you to light swiftly
on dark earth; then, blissful one,

smiling your immortal smile
you asked, What ailed me now that
made me call you again? What

was it that my distracted
heart most wanted? "Whom has
Persuasion to bring round now

"to your love? Who, Sappho, is
unfair to you? For, let her
run, she will soon run after;

"if she won't accept gifts, she
will one day give them; and if
she won't love you—she soon will

"love, although unwillingly. . . ."
If ever—come now! Relieve
this intolerable pain!

What my heart most hopes will
happen, make happen; you your-
self join forces on my side!

He is more than a hero

He is a god in my eyes—
the man who is allowed
to sit beside you—he

who listens intimately
to the sweet murmur of
your voice, the enticing

laughter that makes my own
heart beat fast. If I meet
you suddenly, I can't

speak—my tongue is broken;
a thin flame runs under
my skin; seeing nothing,

hearing only my own ears
drumming, I drip with sweat;
trembling shakes my body

and I turn paler than
dry grass. At such times
death isn't far from me

                                        Even in Sardis
Anactoria will think often of us

of the life we shared here, when you seemed
the Goddess incarnate
to her and your singing pleased her best

Now among Lydian women she in her
turn stands first as the red-
fingered moon rising at sunset takes

precedence over stars around her;
her light spreads equally
on the salt sea and fields thick with bloom

Delicious dew pours down to freshen
roses, delicate thyme
and blossoming sweet clover; she wanders

aimlessly, thinking of gentle
Atthis, her heart hanging
heavy with longing in her little breast

She shouts aloud, Come! we know it;
thousand-eared night repeats that cry
across the sea shining between us

To an army wife, in Sardis:

Some say a cavalry corps,
some infantry, some, again,
will maintain that the swift oars

of our fleet are the finest
sight on dark earth; but I say
that whatever one loves, is.

This is easily proved: did
not Helen—she who had scanned
the flower of the world's manhood—

choose as first among men one
who laid Troy's honor in ruin?
warped to his will, forgetting

love due her own blood, her own
child, she wandered far with him.
So Anactoria, although you

being far away forget us,
the dear sound of your footstep
and light glancing in your eyes

would move me more than glitter
of Lydian horse or armored
tread of mainland infantry

I have had not one word from her

Frankly I wish I were dead.
When she left, she wept

a great deal; she said to
me, "This parting must be
endured, Sappho. I go unwillingly."

I said, "Go, and be happy
but remember (you know
well) whom you leave shackled by love

"If you forget me, think
of our gifts to Aphrodite
and all the loveliness that we shared

"all the violet tiaras,
braided rosebuds, dill and
crocus twined around your young neck

"myrrh poured on your head
and on soft mats girls with
all that they most wished for beside them

"while no voices chanted
choruses without ours,
no woodlot bloomed in spring with-
          out song . . ."

　　　It was you, Atthis, who said

"Sappho, if you will not get
up and let us look at you
I shall never love you again!

"Get up, unleash your suppleness,
lift off your Chian nightdress
and, like a lily leaning into

"a spring, bathe in the water.
Cleis is bringing your best
purple frock and the yellow

"tunic down from the clothes chest;
you will have a cloak thrown over
you and flowers crowning your hair . . .

"Praxinoa, my child, will you please
roast nuts for our breakfast? One
of the gods is being good to us:

"today we are going at last
into Mitylene, our favorite
city, with Sappho, loveliest

"of its women; she will walk
among us like a mother with
all her daughters around her

"when she comes home from exile . . ."

But you forget everything

PART FOUR

፴ 44   Without warning

As a whirlwind
swoops on an oak
Love shakes my heart

፴ 45   If you will come

I shall put out
new pillows for
you to rest on

Thank you, my dear

You came, and you did
well to come: I needed
you. You have made

love blaze up in
my breast—bless you!
Bless you as often

as the hours have
been endless to me
while you were gone

I was so happy

        Believe me, I
        prayed that that
        night might be
        doubled for us

Now I know why Eros,

        Of all the progeny of
        Earth and Heaven, has
        been most dearly loved

回 49   She was dressed well:

Her feet were hidden
under embroidered
sandal straps—fine
handwork from Asia

*her kindness & beuty are
hidden onder a not so
beutifoll body*

回 50   But you, monkey face

Atthis, I loved you
long ago while you
still seemed to me a
small ungracious child

℗ 51   I was proud of you, too

In skill I think
you need never
bow to any girl

not one who may
see the sunlight
in time to come

℗ 52   After all this

Atthis, you hate
even the thought

of me. You dart
off to Andromeda

॥ 53

With his venom

Irresistible
and bittersweet

that loosener
of limbs, Love

reptile-like
strikes me down

Afraid of losing you

I ran fluttering
like a little girl
after her mother

画 55   It is clear now:

Neither honey nor
the honey bee is
to be mine again

画 56   Day in, day out

I hunger and
I struggle

回 57   You will say

See, I have come
back to the soft
arms I turned from
in the old days

回 58   Tell me

Out of all
mankind, whom
do you love

Better than
you love me?

I said, Sappho

Enough! Why
try to move
a hard heart?

You may forget but

Let me tell you
this: someone in
some future time
will think of us

回 61   Pain penetrates

Me drop
by drop

· 🄿 PART FIVE

The nightingale's

The soft-spoken
announcer of
Spring's presence

Last night

I dreamed that
you and I had
words: Cyprian

Tonight I've watched

The moon and then
the Pleiades
go down

The night is now
half-gone; youth
goes; I am

in bed alone

℞ 65   Persuasion

Aphrodite's
daughter, you
cheat mortals

℞ 66   Many's the time

I've wished I, O
gold-crowned
Aphrodite,
had luck like that

回 67　　　At my age

Why does the swallow
of heaven, daughter
of King Pandion,
bring news to plague me?

回 68　　　That was different

My girlhood then
was in full bloom
and you—

ဩ 69   This way, that way

          I do not know
          what to do: I
          am of two minds

ဩ 70   My lovely friends

          How could I change
          towards you who
          are so beautiful?

௴ 71   I ask you, sir, to

        Stand face to face
        with me as a friend
        would: show me the
        favor of your eyes

௴ 72   Of course I love you

        But if you love me,
        marry a young woman!

        I couldn't stand it
        to live with a young
        man, I being older

Yes, it is pretty

But come, dear, need
you pride yourself
that much on a ring?

I hear that Andromeda—

That hayseed in her hay-
seed finery—has put
a torch to your heart

and she without even
the art of lifting her
skirt over her ankles

ꀅ 75   Well!

Andromeda has
got herself a
fair exchange

ꀅ 76   Sappho, when some fool

Explodes rage
in your breast
hold back that
yapping tongue!

⊡ 77   Strange to say

Those whom I treated
well are those who do
me the most injury now

⊡ 78   I taught the talented

And furthermore, I did
well in instructing
Hero, who was a girl
track star from Gyara

Really, Gorgo,

My disposition
is not at all
spiteful: I have
a childlike heart

As you love me

Cypris, make her
find even you too
bitter! Make her

stop her loud-mouthed
bragging: "See, twice
now, Doricha

"has arrived at
just such love
as she wanted!"

Greetings to Gorgo

I salute, madam,

the descendant of
many great kings

a great many times

Rich as you are

Death will finish
you: afterwards no
one will remember

or want you: you
had no share in
the Pierian roses

You will flitter
invisible among
the indistinct dead
in Hell's palace
darting fitfully

Don't ask me what to wear

I have no embroidered
headband from Sardis to
give you, Cleis, such as
I wore
         and my mother
always said that in her
day a purple ribbon
looped in the hair was thought
to be high style indeed

but we were dark:
                    a girl
whose hair is yellower than
torchlight should wear no
headdress but fresh flowers

PART SIX

ⵣ 84   If you are squeamish

Don't prod the
beach rubble

℞ 85   Before they were mothers

Leto and Niobe
had been the most
devoted of friends

℞ 86   Experience shows us

Wealth unchaperoned
by Virtue is never
an innocuous neighbor

weath w/o virtue is dangerous

℞ 87   We know this much

Death is an evil;
we have the gods'
word for it; they too
would die if death
were a good thing

℞ 88   Say what you please

Gold is God's child;
neither worms nor
moths eat gold; it
is much stronger
than a man's heart

◩ 89　　　Then the god of war

Ares, boasted to us
that he could haul off
Hephaistos, master of
the Forges, by sheer force

◩ 90　　　As for the exiles

I think they had
never found you,
Peace, more diffi-
cult to endure!

ꗞ 91   In memory

         Of Pelagon, a fisherman,
         his father Meniscus placed

         here a fishbasket and oar:
         tokens of an unlucky life

ꗞ 92   Do you remember

         How a golden
         broom grows on
         the sea beaches

Be kind to me

Gongyla; I ask only
that you wear the cream
white dress when you come

Desire darts about your
loveliness, drawn down in
circling flight at sight of it

and I am glad, although
once I too quarrelled
with Aphrodite
                    to whom
I pray that you will
come soon

₪ 94   You remind me

Of a very gentle
little girl I once
watched picking flowers

₪ 95   When they were tired

Night rained her
thick dark sleep
upon their eyes

The gods bless you

May you sleep then
on some tender
girl friend's breast

I have often asked you
not to come now

Hermes, Lord, you
who lead the ghosts
home:
        But this time
I am not happy; I
want to die, to see
the moist lotus open
along Acheron

℞ 98   It is the Muses

Who have caused me
to be honored: they
taught me their craft

.

℞ 99   Must I remind you, Cleis,

That sounds of grief
are unbecoming in
a poet's household?

and that they are not
suitable in ours?

I have no complaint

Prosperity that
the golden Muses
gave me was no
delusion: dead, I
won't be forgotten

A FOOTNOTE

TO THESE TRANSLATIONS

Lesbos in the seventh and sixth centuries B.C. considered itself the very fountainhead of Greek song. Sappho was not, as has sometimes been assumed by those unacquainted with the tradition, a lonely poet adrift on a provincial island. The Greek-speaking world had no capital city, but Mitylene and the neighboring cities along the coast of Asia Minor—Phocaea, Miletus, Ephesus, and Smyrna—were among the richest and liveliest Greek settlements of that period. In the islands lying south of Lesbos off the Asia Minor coast—those which we call the Dodecanese—both art and science were flourishing. This was the age which produced the Hera of Samos and the Pythagorean philosophers.

Sappho was "early" if you consider Periclean Athens the peak towards which Greek civilization was tending, but this of course is a point of view which could never have occurred to her. She was riding the crest of her own wave; her world seemed as modern to her as ours does to us, and just about as troubled. Furthermore, her view of it was not limited. She must have known Egypt and Babylon by hearsay and perhaps even Marseilles, since the city of Phocaea had already established its colony there. If the tradition that she spent a period of exile in Syracuse is based on fact, she knew Sicily at first hand. She is said to have been exiled by the tyrant Pittacus for political reasons; nevertheless, if we may judge by the surviving poems, what interested her most was her private life and her poetry. In these interests she is not untypical of women and poets generally.

The biographical tradition,[1] which is full of contradictions, says further:

That she was born in Mitylene, or in Eresus on the same island;

That her birth date was about 612 B.C., or earlier, or later;

That her father's name was Scamandronymous, or Eurygyus, or Simon, or Eunominus, or Euarchus, or Ecrytus, or Semus;

That her mother's name was Cleis;

That she married a merchant of Andros, named Cercolas, and had a daughter Cleis; or, contrariwise, that Cercolas is a fictitious name, and that Cleis was not her daughter;

That she had three brothers, one being Charaxus, who incurred the displeasure of his sister when he purchased the freedom of a courtesan named Doricha;

---

[1] Most of the gossip is quoted and discussed by J. M. Edmonds in *Lyra Graeca*, Vol. I (Loeb Classical Library, 1922 and 1928).

That Sappho herself was a prostitute; that she was not;

That, maddened by her hopeless love for Phaon, a ferryman, she threw herself from the Leucadian cliffs (on an island lying between Ithaca and Corfu); or, contrariwise, that she died at home in bed, tended by her daughter, Cleis (see poem 99);

That the girls whose names are mentioned in the poems—Anactoria, Atthis, Gongyla, Hero, Timas— were her pupils, and participants with her in the religious exercises of *kallichoron* Mitylene (Mitylene of the beautiful dances); or, conversely, that they were no such thing.

Most of this material is irrelevant to the reading and enjoyment of her poems in any case. We do not need to know her father's name or her husband's. The dispute about Cleis is more serious because of the references to her in the poems. I have assumed that when Sappho said "daughter" she meant "daughter." All the references to Cleis seem to fit in with that assumption.

The charge of prostitution is usually dismissed by modern scholars as a myth originating in the good-natured fun of Athenian comic poets. The tale about the Leucadian cliffs is seldom taken seriously nowadays. The final argument, that concerning Sappho's role as priestess and pedagogue, has a considerable bearing on the reading and translation of the poems. Unfortunately it is far from being settled. The case *for* has been stated by many scholars, including Sir

Maurice Bowra. The case *against* has been recently and roundly stated by Denys L. Page in terms which have completely convinced some of his readers.

Bowra says in his essay on Sappho:

She was the leader and chief personality in an institution which trained young girls, but owing to the customs of the time this institution had a special character. It was, as she herself calls it, a *moisopolōn domos,* a house of those who cultivated the Muses. But it was much more than a school or an occasional association of girls for religious purposes. It was primarily concerned with the cult of Aphrodite, and its members formed a *thiasos,* resembling that at Eresus, which excluded men from its number, or the company of women on Paros united in the cult of Aphrodite Oistro. Sappho's *thiasos* was not the only one of its kind in Mitylene. Others were controlled by her rivals, Gorgo and Andromeda, and Sappho's relations with them were not of the friendliest character. The members of the *thiasos* were bound to each other and to their leader by ties of great strength and intimacy, and Maximus of Tyre was not far wrong when he compared the relations between Sappho and her pupils with those between Socrates and his disciples. But while Socrates held his young men together by his personal influence and the glamour he gave to the quest for truth, Sappho was bound to her maidens by ties which were at least half religious. . . .

A *thiasos* of this kind cannot really be considered in its proper aspect if we judge it by the standards of the modern world. Its cult was not a self-conscious aestheticism but a genuine worship of a goddess in whom all believed. . . . The Muses were honored with Aphrodite. It was felt that her ceremonies de-

manded songs, and in song her devotees were trained
by Sappho. . . .[2]

Professor Page rejects both the *thiasos* and the
moisopolōn domos. He says:

> It is clear and certain that the themes of the great
> majority of extant fragments are the loves and the
> jealousies, the pleasures and pains, of Sappho and
> her companions. We have found, and shall find, no
> trace of any formal or official or professional rela-
> tionship between them: no trace of Sappho the
> priestess of a cult association, Sappho the principal of
> an academy; with feigned solemnity we exorcise
> these melancholy modern ghosts.[3]

He does, however, accept the remark of Maximus
of Tyre which compares the positions of Socrates
and Sappho; he also agrees, as regards the girls, that
"They come from Miletus, from Phocaea, from Colo-
phon, to live in Sappho's society; and one day they go
away again." This he calls a "commonplace" situation,
though it seems to me unparalleled, and altogether
more remarkable than the *thiasos* described above,
remarkable as that is. Andromeda, he says, is the
"leader of a company of young women," a rival like
Gorgo; presumably, then, young girls are sent to[4]

---

[2] C. M. Bowra, *Greek Lyric Poetry* (Oxford, 1936), pp. 187–189.
(There is a great deal more of this.)

[3] Denys L. Page, *Sappho and Alcaeus* (Oxford, 1955), pp. 139–
140. (There is a great deal more of this, too.)

[4] Professor Page might object to "sent to"; however, although a
number of scholars are agreed that the women of Lesbos and
Miletus may have had greater freedom than Athenian women, no
one has ever suggested that young unmarried girls had money to
spend as they liked and freedom to travel where they pleased.

them also, from the islands and from Greek cities
along the Asia Minor coast, yet there is no formal
relationship, and no trace of a religious cult:

> . . . the theory finds no support whatever in any-
> thing worthy of the name of fact. External sources
> help it not at all: the search must be limited to the
> surviving fragments of Sappho's poetry. And there
> we find nothing that suggests, let alone enforces, the
> recognition of a priestess or the principal of an
> academy.[5]

To the phrase "external sources" he appends the
following astonishing footnote:

> The copious but inane biographical tradition offers
> nothing more valuable than the word *mathetriai* in
> Suidas: certain girls, according to this, were "pupils"
> of Sappho; this need mean no more than that Sappho
> taught her friends the tricks of her poetic trade
> (*96.5* [my 40]). Atthis was herself a singer.

In translating and annotating these poems I have
followed Bowra. I myself should prefer, however, to
compare Sappho's entirely hypothetical position to
that of *kapelmeister,* or perhaps to that of a Renais-
sance painter with a studio full of talented young
fellows picking up the tricks of painting altarpieces.
The phrase "principal of an academy" makes the
whole theory absurd, as, of course, Professor Page in-
tended. In the end he seems to agree on essentials if
not on the romantic overtones. His insistence that we
have no evidence of a *formal* relationship, may mean
simply that we have found no signed contracts, arti-

[5] Page, *op. cit.,* p. 111 and footnote 2.

cles of apprenticeship or licenses to teach. The scholar who deciphers fragments of illegible writing on a papyrus two thousand years old is subject to a discipline which requires him to reject any assumption not forced on him by the evidence before his eyes. That is as it should be. However, when we come to consider the sense of the poetry and the human relationships, we should, I feel, have the privilege of tentatively rejecting any theory which outrages common sense, and tentatively accepting one which clarifies an otherwise incomprehensible picture, whether the theory we accept is forced upon us by the textual evidence or not.

The surprising number of women poets[6] in sixth-century Greece suggests that for some reason people thought it advisable for young women to study and practice the composition of poetry and music. The choruses of girls dancing and singing at festivals in honor of Artemis and Aphrodite suggest a possible reason for this unusual attitude, namely, the use of songs in religious exercises, some of which were performed exclusively by and for women. We know that Alcman trained and wrote for choruses of girls in Sparta, and we have good reason to assume that Sappho performed the same service for her native city. Alcman, it is said, was brought from Sardis to Sparta to fill this role of *kapelmeister,* but local talent must often have been employed; and the parents of ambitious young girls who aspired to the position might,

[6] Even one woman poet would be surprising. We hear, however, of a number of them, including Corinna of Thebes, who is said to have taught Pindar the tricks of *his* trade.

in that case, have been moved to send them to study
with the most celebrated lyricist of the day if she
were willing to accept them as students, companions,
apprentices, novices, or whatever word may be con-
sidered appropriate. On this hypothesis an otherwise
inexplicable situation becomes understandable even if
some aspects of it strike us as highly unusual.

2

These translations were undertaken, first of all, for
my own pleasure and instruction. I have also tried, for
the benefit of those who do not read Greek, to convey
some of the qualities of the original which earlier
translations do not carry over—at least to the modern
ear. I could hardly expect to reproduce all the virtues
of a poem by Sappho in an English translation. The
flexibility of Greek allows complicated tense structure
and swift movement at the same moment. The am-
biguities which enrich her simplest lines, the over-
tones and undertones, the occasional puns, which are
not quite puns and seem right instead of ridiculous,
are almost impossible to convey in another language.
Besides, I would have to be technically as expert as
she was in order to approximate the music of her
poetry.

Of all her virtues, however, the one most stressed by
her modern critics and least taken account of by her
translators is that of fresh colloquial directness of
speech. Bowra says:

> The sense of her poems goes naturally with the
> meter and seems to fall into it, so that it looks like
> ordinary speech raised to the highest level of ex-
> pressiveness. In her great range of different meters
> there is not one which does not move with perfect
> ease and receive her words as if they were ordained
> for it.[7]

I should say, rather: as if she had invented it in that
moment for that phrase alone.

This style of writing, which she brought to its
greatest perfection, was peculiar to her age, and to
the Aeolian lyric tradition. The writers in the iambic
meter used speech cadence, but their songs were not
sung to the accompaniment of the lyre, and so they
are not, strictly speaking, lyricists. Pindar, on the
other hand, belonged to a tradition in which per-
sonal expression was no longer important. Before
he died, the lyrical tradition itself had been super-
seded by tragedy, and the impersonal lyric had be-
come the chorus.

Every translator of poetry has to face and solve
somehow the problem of "that which is untranslat-
able." The translator of Sappho has to cope with
serious textual problems in addition. The texts vary to
such an extent and have been emended by so many
hands that the translator has a choice of words and
meanings for almost every line. Such problems often
arise out of the circumstances of survival. The sources
for our texts are various, and most of them are as
unsatisfactory as might be expected in the case of a

[7] Bowra, *op. cit.,* p. 246.

poet who lived twenty-five centuries ago. Sappho may or may not have written her poems down. She sang or recited them with lyre accompaniment; they were passed on to professional singers who sang them wherever Greek was spoken. Copies were made and these copies were copied. The earliest papyrus text we possess dates from the third century B.C., about three hundred years after her death. Copyists were not always reliable, so that different texts sometimes offer choices of words, when we are fortunate enough to have two texts.

Papyrus books were long rolls of a kind of durable paper made from the stalks of a water plant. The poems were written crosswise of the roll, in capitals because lower case had not yet been invented. Punctuation marks and Greek accents, which often determine the meaning of a word to the modern scholar, are also lacking. When a sentence is incomplete, or only possibly complete, the absence of these guides to reading becomes more serious. Greek construction allows considerable freedom in the placing of words—adjectives for instance—and the punctuation placed by the modern scholar who edits the text may establish which noun the adjective modifies. These difficulties are added to what appears to be a deliberate use of ambiguity, as in the placing of "gold" where it modifies either the chariot of Aphrodite or the home of her father.

The papyrus scrolls were eventually torn into strips, crosswise of the roll, lengthwise of the poem, and pasted together to form cartonage coffins. Other papyri have been found, torn into strips, on rubbish heaps, and other strips were wadded and stuffed into the mouths of mummified crocodiles. The tearing into strips has meant that we have, of the poems which survive only on papyrus, the middles of some lines, both ends of others, and some half lines, but almost no complete lines. This is the case with a good many poems which I have not tried to translate. Other fragments have been preserved by grammarians who quoted a phrase to illustrate a special use of the negative, a grammatical error, or the Aeolian form of a noun ending in o. Still others were preserved by literary critics who quoted passages as examples of the felicity of her style, or her use of (for instance) the antispastic brachycatalectic trimeter variation of *ionic a majore* meter. Dionysius of Halicarnassus quoted the whole of the Ode to Aphrodite. Longinus quoted what is probably all of poem 39. Most of their colleagues, confident that their readers would have all her poems well in mind, merely referred to "the poem in which Sappho says" with perhaps a line or two of quotation. Other morsels were cited to illustrate points made by an orator, an antiquarian, or a historian. Aristotle quoted fragment 87.

In translating these poems, I have been careful to put into first lines, set off as titles, the supplementary phrases which are sometimes taken from the context in which the fragment was quoted, sometimes supplied by me for the sake of elucidation, as a setting for the tiny fragment, or as a conjecture to supply the sense of missing lines. Wherever the text is taken from a tattered papyrus, I have usually preferred to condense instead of filling in the gaps, although here and there it has seemed better to guess at a word or accept the guess of some scholar. I have made minor grammatical changes whenever I had what seemed a good reason for them; and I have added here and there a phrase descriptive of the function of a god or goddess who is less familiar to the modern reader than Aphrodite. As for the music, I have done what I could. The sin which I have been most careful to avoid is that of spinning the fragment out "to make a poem." What is there, with the exceptions which I have noted, is what Sappho said, or at any rate what they say she said.

MARY BARNARD

▣ NOTES

In the following notes "E." followed by a number indicates the
number of the poem or fragment in Edmonds (see bibliography).
The Greek text, full notes on sources, and fairly literal translations
will be found in that volume. This is the text I have used unless
I have indicated otherwise.

1. Athenaeus, *Doctors at Dinner*. E. 12.
2. Treatise on Etymology. E. 18.

PART ONE
3. Ammonius, citing grammatical error. E. 19.
4. Hephaestion, on metric. E. 126.
5. Apollonius, on pronouns. E. 7.
6. Athenaeus (*see* 1). E. 118.
7. Demetrius, literary criticism. E. 94.
8. Hermogenes, literary criticism. E. 80.
9. The text of this fragment is from a vase painting; the last
   word is illegible. E. 1a. *See* Haines, 1, and plate 12.
10. Scholiast on Aristophanes. E. 67.
11. Hephaestion (*see* 4). E. 103.
12. The same. E. 135, including note 2.
13. Treatise on Etymology. E. 97. Text from Wharton, 56.
14. Athenaeus (*see* 1). E. 146.
15. Pollux, on vocabulary. E. 69. Text from Wharton, 64.
16. Demetrius (*see* 7). E. 149.
17. Hephaestion (*see* 4). E. 130.
18. The same. E. 115.
19. Athenaeus (*see* 1). E. 117.
20. Palatine Anthology. This is probably complete. E. 144, in-
    cluding note.
21. Athenaeus (*see* 1), speaking of head kerchiefs. E. 87.

22. Hephaestion (*see* 4). E. 112.
23. The same. E. 114.
24. Eustathius, literary criticism. E. 3.
25. Hephaestion (*see* 4). E. 101.

PART TWO

26. Himerius, an oration. E. 32.
27. Himerius, an epithalamium. E. 157.
28. Annotator of Theocritus. E. 68.
29. Demetrius (*see* 7). E. 148.
30. Hephaestion (*see* 4) and Choricius, *Epithalamy of Zachary*. E. 155, 156, and 158.
31. Himerius, an epithalamium. E. 147.
32. Demetrius (*see* 7). E. 164.
33. Hephaestion (*see* 4). E. 154.
34. Annotator of Hermogenes, a literary critic, and Demetrius (*see* 7). E. 150, 151.
35. Philodemus on *Piety*. E. 24.
36. Apollonius, on conjunctions. E. 159.

PART THREE

37. E. 4, 6. Text from Page, 3; and Quasimodo, p. 29 and note pp. 156–158.
38. Dionysius of Halicarnassus, literary criticism. E. 1.
39. Longinus, *On the Sublime*. E. 2.
40. A manuscript dating from the 7th century A.D. E. 86. Page rejects the last three lines.
41. From a 2nd century papyrus. E. 38. Page has published a somewhat different but still unsatisfactory version of the central portion of the poem. *See also* Haines, 11.
42. From the same manuscript as 40. E. 83.
43. From the reverse of 42. E. 82. Edmonds warns that this poem is "very tentatively restored." Page and Bowra do not include it among poems quoted by them.

PART FOUR

44. Maximus of Tyre, essayist. E. 54.
45. Herodian, grammarian. E. 56.
46. An Epistle of Julian, the last Pagan emperor. E. 89.
47. Libanius, *Orations*. E. 84 A.
48. Scholiasts on Theocritus and Apollonius Rhodius. E. 31.
49. A commentator on Aristophanes. E. 20 and note. Text *see also* Wharton, 19.
50. Hephaestion (*see* 4) and Plutarch, *Amatorius*. E. 48.
51. Chrysippus, a grammarian. E. 72.
52. Hephaestion (*see* 4). E. 81.
53. The same. E. 81.

54. Herodian (*see* 45). E. 142.
55. Diogenian, on proverbs. E. 106.
56. Treatise on Etymology. E. 23.
57. Herodian (*see* 45). E. 96. There are as many readings of this fragment as there are editors. *See,* besides Edmonds, Wharton, 55, and Haines, 49.
58. Apollonius, on pronouns. E. 22.
59. Herodian (*see* 45). E. 93.
60. Dio Chrysostom, *Discourses.* E. 76.
61. Treatise on Etymology. The author says that Sappho used the word *stalagmon,* a constant dripping, of pain. E. 17.

PART FIVE

62. Commentator on Sophocles. E. 138.
63. Hephaestion (*see* 4). E. 123.
64. The same. E. 111. Several editors have denied that this is by Sappho.
65. Commentator on Hesiod. E. 33.
66. Apollonius, on syntax. E. 9.
67. Hephaestion (*see* 4). E. 122.
68. Terentius Maurus, on metric. E. 48. This is not certainly by Sappho.
69. Chrysippus, grammarian. E. 52.
70. Apollonius (*see* 5). E. 14.
71. Athenaeus (*see* 1). E. 120.
72. Stobaeus, anthologist. E. 99.
73. Herodian (*see* 45). E. 51.
74. Athenaeus (*see* 1). E. 98.
75. Hephaestion (*see* 4). E. 125.
76. Plutarch, essayist. E. 137.
77. Treatise on Etymology. E. 13.
78. Aldus, grammarian. E. 73.
79. Treatise on Etymology. E. 74.
80. From a 2nd century papyrus. E. 37.
81. Maximus of Tyre, essayist. E. 121.
82. Stobaeus, anthologist. E. 71. Plutarch tells us that this fragment was written to a "wealthy woman" of "no refinement or learning." My text, from Quasimodo, 58.
83. From recently discovered 3rd century papyrus. Not in Edmonds. Text from Page, 11.

PART SIX

84. Commentator on Apollonius of Rhodes. E. 78.
85. Athenaeus (*see* 1). E. 140.
86. Scholiast on Pindar. E. 100.
87. Aristotle, *On Rhetoric.* E. 91.

88. Scholiast on Pindar. This has also been attributed to Pindar. E. 110.
89. Priscian, grammarian. E. 70.
90. Hephaestion (*see* 4). E. 116.
91. Palatine Anthology. E. 145. The attribution of this fragment to Sappho has been questioned.
92. Athenaeus (*see* 1). E. 139.
93. From a 2nd century papyrus. E. 45.
94. Athenaeus (*see* 1). E. 107.
95. Apollonius, on pronouns. E. 141.
96. Treatise on Etymology. E. 128.
97. From a 7th century manuscript. E. 85.
98. Apollonius, a grammarian. E. 10.
99. Maximus of Tyre, essayist, who says Sappho addressed her daughter in these words, and compares them with those of Socrates when he was about to die. E. 108.
100. Aristides, rhetorician. E. 11.

▣ BIBLIOGRAPHY

Bowra, C. M. *Greek Lyric Poetry*. Oxford, 1936.
  Text of many poems, and excellent critical comment.
Edmonds, J. M. *Lyra Graeca,* Vol. I. (Loeb Classical Library)
  London, 1922 and 1928.
  Text and literal translations in English.
Haines, C. R. *Sappho. The Poems and Fragments*. London and
  New York [1926].
  Text and translations, with many illustrations from coins, vase
  paintings, and sculpture.
Page, Denys L. *Sappho and Alcaeus*. Oxford, 1955.
  Text and translations of twelve poems and a few fragments,
  with criticism.
Quasimodo, Salvatore. *Lyrici Greci*. (Biblioteca Moderna Monda-
  dori) Milan, 1951.
  Greek text of selected poems with translations into Italian
  verse.
Weigall, Arthur. *Sappho of Lesbos*. Garden City, 1932.
  Biography and background, with translations scattered through
  the narrative.
Wharton, Henry Thornton. *Sappho*. London, 1885.
  Memoir, text, and selected renderings. The standard work in
  English until Edmonds' *Lyra Graeca,* it lacks the recent dis-
  coveries. Comprehensive bibliography lists translations into
  French, German, Spanish, and Italian.

ꝏ DESCRIPTIVE INDEX

References are to poem numbers.

Eros, the god of love, the young attendant of Aphrodite, 15, 48

Gongyla, one of Sappho's pupils, 93

Gorgo, a woman who is said to have been wealthy and a rival of Sappho's, 79, 81; 82 is probably also addressed to Gorgo.

Graces, the companions of Aphrodite, whose names may be translated by the words "Gaiety," "Revelry," and "Radiance," 19, 25, 27, 28, 30

Gyara, an island in the Cyclades, 78

Gyrinno, one of Sappho's pupils, said to be a favorite, 18

Hecate, an ancient goddess of the night, and of enchanters, 35

Helen, queen of Sparta, 41

Hephaistos, the blacksmith god, forger of weapons and armor, 89

Hera, wife of Zeus and patroness of marriage, 31

Hermes, according to Sappho, the cupbearer of the gods, 14; as the *psychopompus,* the god who guides the dead to the underworld, 97

Hero, one of Sappho's pupils, 78

Hesperus, the evening star, 16, 31

Leda, a Spartan princess who was seduced by Zeus in the form of a swan; she gave birth to Helen and her twin brothers who are said to have been hatched from an egg; according to one story, Nemesis, the goddess of vengeance, laid the egg, and Leda only found it. 13

Leto, mother of Apollo and Artemis (*see* Niobe), 85

Lydia, the chief kingdom of Asia Minor, ruled in Sappho's day by Alyattes and his son Croesus, 40, 41

Meniscus, father of Pelagon, 91

Mitylene (also spelled Mytilene), Sappho's home during most of her life, 43

Mnasidica, one of Sappho's pupils, 18, 19

Muses, the nine divine patrons of the arts, 25, 98, 100

Niobe, mother of fifty (or seven) sons and the same number of daughters; she made the mistake of bragging to Leto about the number of her children. While Leto had only one son and one daughter, they were powerful deities who promptly killed all of Niobe's children to avenge the insult to their mother. 85

Pandion, a legendary king of Athens, whose daughter was changed into a swallow; swallows proverbially carried messages and announced the spring. 67

Paphos, a town of Cyprus, one of the earliest and most important centers of worship of Aphrodite, 31